UNUSUAL LiFE CYCLES OF

AMPHIBIANS

by Jaclyn Jaycox

CAPSTONE PRESS
a capstone imprint

Capstone Captivate is published by Capstone Press, an imprint of Capstone.
1710 Roe Crest Drive
North Mankato, Minnesota 56003
www.capstonepub.com

Library of Congress Cataloging-in-Publication Data is available on the Library of Congress website.
ISBN: 978-1-4966-9535-2 (hardcover)
ISBN: 978-1-4966-9700-4 (paperback)
ISBN: 978-1-9771-5521-4 (eBook PDF)

Summary: Have you ever heard of a frog that freezes solid in winter? What about a toad that carries its eggs on its back? Young readers will learn all about wood frogs, Surinam toads, and other amphibians with unusual life cycles.

Image Credits
Minden Pictures/Ryu Uchiyama, 19; Newscom/ANT/NHPA/Photoshot, 13; Science Source: Dante Fenolio, 27, ER Degginger, 9, Robert Noonan, 17, The Natural History Museum, London, 25; Shutterstock: almondd, 21, Arm001, 15, Christopher Unsworth, 29, Dan Olsen, 11, Jakinnboaz, 7, kamnuan, cover, Matteo photos, 5, Michael Benard, 23

Design elements: Shutterstock: emEF, Max Krasnov

Editorial Credits
Editor: Gena Chester; Designer: Bobbie Nuytten; Media Researcher: Kelly Garvin; Production Specialist: Laura Manthe

All internet sites appearing in back matter were available and accurate when this book was sent to press.

Words in **bold** are in the glossary.

Printed and bound in China. PO4205

Table of Contents

CHAPTER 1
Amphibian Life Cycle

Hop! Hop! Hop! Look at that frog jumping through the grass. Can you believe it didn't even have legs when it was born? Frogs are **amphibians**. These animals go through amazing transformations from birth to adulthood.

Most amphibians have similar life cycles. They change from eggs to **larvae** and then to adults. Let's take a look at frogs. They start out life in the water. A female frog lays eggs in a pond. It leaves the eggs somewhere hidden. Female frogs don't care for their eggs. Hiding them is their best chance for survival. Tadpoles hatch from these eggs. They don't look like adult frogs. They have tails and no legs. They breathe through **gills**. They live in the water as they grow.

a frog with its eggs

Soon the tadpoles begin a big change called **metamorphosis**. First, they grow back legs. They eat **algae** and other tiny plants. Then their front legs start to grow. Their tails get shorter. Skin grows over their gills. After about 12 weeks, the frogs' transformations are complete. They are now adult frogs and ready for life on land.

Although most amphibians have similar life cycles, there are some animals that grow very differently. Some lay eggs on land instead of in water. Others don't go through metamorphosis. And some have unique features that can help them survive life in the wild. Let's take a look at some amphibians with unusual life cycles.

Fact!

Frogs, toads, and salamanders are amphibians. Newts are too.

A FROG'S LIFE CYCLE

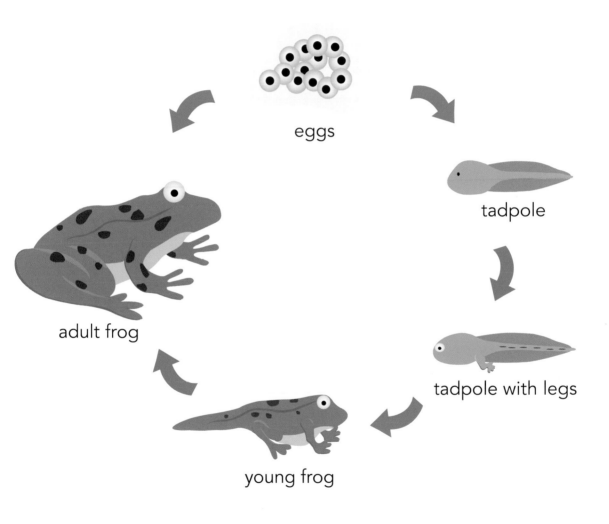

eggs

tadpole

tadpole with legs

young frog

adult frog

CHAPTER 2

Unusual Births

Surinam Toads

Surinam toads are different from other amphibians in a couple of ways. They live most of their lives underwater instead of on land. They have flat bodies. Their legs and arms are always stretched out. Under the water, they look like floating pieces of wood or leaves. This makes it hard for **predators** to see them.

Like some other water animals, Surinam toads don't have tongues. They catch their **prey** by opening their mouths wide and sucking them in. They can't breathe underwater. But these toads can hold their breath for a long time. They can go an hour without coming to the surface for air.

a Surinam toad

The female Surinam toad lays between 60 and 100 eggs. The male pushes the eggs up onto the female's back. The eggs stick there. The female's skin begins to grow, forming pockets around the eggs. After a few days, the skin has completely covered the eggs. The eggs hatch, but stay under the skin for about four months. Eggs and tadpoles have a lot of predators. By growing under their mother's skin, they have a much better chance of survival.

The tadpoles grow into young toads. Then they are ready to live life on their own. The young toads break free from the female's skin. They head to the water's surface to breathe. Then they go find food. They can eat small fish, worms, and crustaceans such as shrimp.

a Surinam toad with eggs on its back

Gastric Brooding Frogs

Gastric brooding frogs have unusual births. They're also unusual in a different way. They haven't been seen in the wild since 1985. In 2002, they were classified as extinct. Scientists are trying to bring them back through **cloning** techniques.

Gastric brooding frogs are small and usually gray or brown in color. Females lay up to 25 eggs at a time. But unlike other frogs, the female doesn't leave the eggs to hatch alone. She swallows them! The eggs hatch in her stomach. The tadpoles grow and change. During this time, the mother stops eating. Her **digestive system** shuts down. This keeps her young from being digested like food.

After about six weeks, the tadpoles have grown into froglets. They are ready for life outside of their mother's stomach. The female opens her mouth wide. The froglets shoot up from her stomach and out her mouth. Then they hop away. It can take several days for all the froglets to leave. About four days after they have all gone, the female starts eating again.

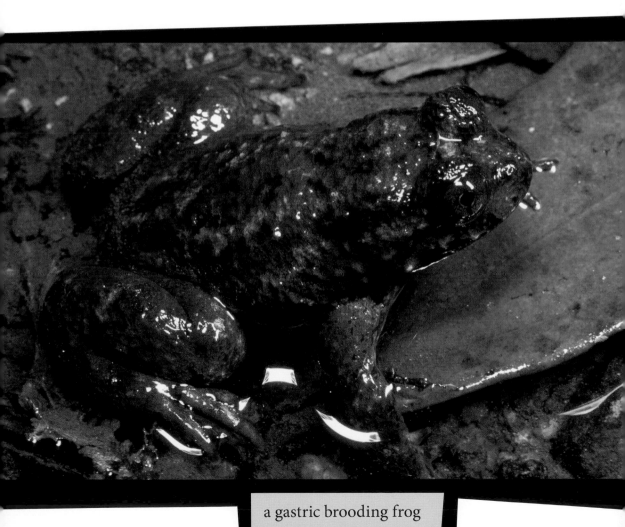

a gastric brooding frog

CHAPTER 3

Unusual Transformations

Axolotl Salamanders

Some amphibians have different ways of growing from babies to adults. One of these animals is the axolotl salamander. The female lays its eggs on rocks and plants at the bottom of a lake. The eggs hatch about two weeks later. The baby salamanders are called larvae.

Larvae look a lot like tadpoles. They have feathery gills on the back of their heads. They grow larger and sprout legs. But unlike other salamanders, they never go through metamorphosis. They grow lungs but rarely use them. They keep their gills and tails. They live in the water their whole lives.

An axolotl salamander larva has gills on its head.

REGROWING LIMBS

Axolotl salamanders can regrow their limbs! If an axolotl loses an arm or leg to a predator, a new one will grow in its place. This animal can also regrow its eyes, spinal cord, and even parts of its brain. Scientists are learning more about how the salamanders do this. One day, scientists may be able to use this information to help people regrow missing limbs.

Hellbenders

Like axolotls, hellbender salamanders live in water as adults. They make their homes in small rivers and streams. The male hellbender builds a nest for the eggs. After the female lays the eggs, the male chases her away. He guards the nest.

Once the eggs hatch, the larvae swim away. They have tails and gills. They grow quickly. In the first year, the larvae double their size. They grow legs with webbed feet. After about two years, hellbenders go through a partial metamorphosis. Their gills close, but they do not use their lungs. They remain underwater animals and breathe through their skin. Hellbenders can live up to 25 years in the wild.

Fact!

Hellbenders are the largest salamanders in North America. They can grow more than 2 feet (0.6 meters) long and weigh more than 4 pounds (1.8 kilograms).

hellbender eggs

Paradoxical Frogs

Like other amphibians, paradoxical frogs hatch from eggs. The tadpoles are small. But they eat and grow very quickly. In the first four months, these tadpoles can grow up to 10 inches (25 centimeters) long. They are about four times bigger than adult paradoxical frogs. As they start to change into froglets, they get smaller. Their long tails start to shrink.

As adults, paradoxical frogs are only about 2 to 3 inches (5 to 8 cm) long. Scientists aren't sure why paradoxical frogs grow this way. Some believe it helps the tadpoles survive. Fewer predators will hunt such large tadpoles.

A paradoxical tadpole can be more than three times as long as adult paradoxical frogs.

Eastern Newts

Eastern newts start out life in the water. They live in lakes and ponds. The larvae hatch from eggs. They have yellowish-brown or green skin. They have gills and long tails. After two to five months, the larvae start to change. Young eastern newts are called red efts. Their skin turns bright red. This color warns predators to stay away. The red efts are poisonous. They grow lungs, legs, and eyelids. Their gills disappear. They move to land and live under leaves.

Eastern newts are fast swimmers. But they are slow on land. Their poisonous skin helps them survive on land.

a red eft on land

Some eastern newts live as red efts for their whole lives. But most live as land animals for two to five years. Then they start to change again. Their skin turns back to yellowish-brown or green. Their tails flatten and become very strong. The eastern newts are now adults. They head back to the water.

Eastern newts spend their adult lives in the water. But they can survive on land if they must. Some ponds dry up in the winter. If this happens, the eastern newts will go underground. They stay there until the rain comes in the spring to fill up the pond. Then they return to the water.

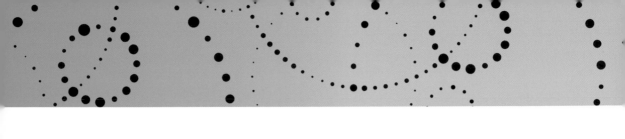

an adult eastern newt

Caecilians

Caecilians look like huge worms. But they are actually amphibians. Caecilians have babies in two ways. Some caecilians lay eggs in wet holes next to water. The larvae hatch from the eggs. Other kinds of caecilians give birth to live young.

Caecilian larvae have short tails and gills. Some caecilian mothers stay with their young. They feed their young, but not like other animals do. The babies eat a layer of the mother's skin.

As the larvae start to change into adults, their skin gets thicker. They grow one lung, and their gills disappear. They also grow **tentacles**. Their tentacles help them find food.

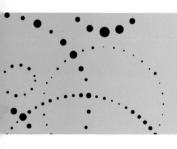

Fact!

Caecilians are the only amphibians that have tentacles.

a caecilian female with her young

When caecilians are adults, they move to land. They live underground. Caecilians are great diggers. Their strong heads and muscles easily tunnel through dirt. Some caecilians have a layer of skin over their eyes. This protects them from the dirt. Their tentacles help them find their way underground.

Caecilians have rows of sharp teeth. They eat worms, small snakes, lizards, and frogs. They swallow their prey whole. Their skin is poisonous. It helps protect them from predators.

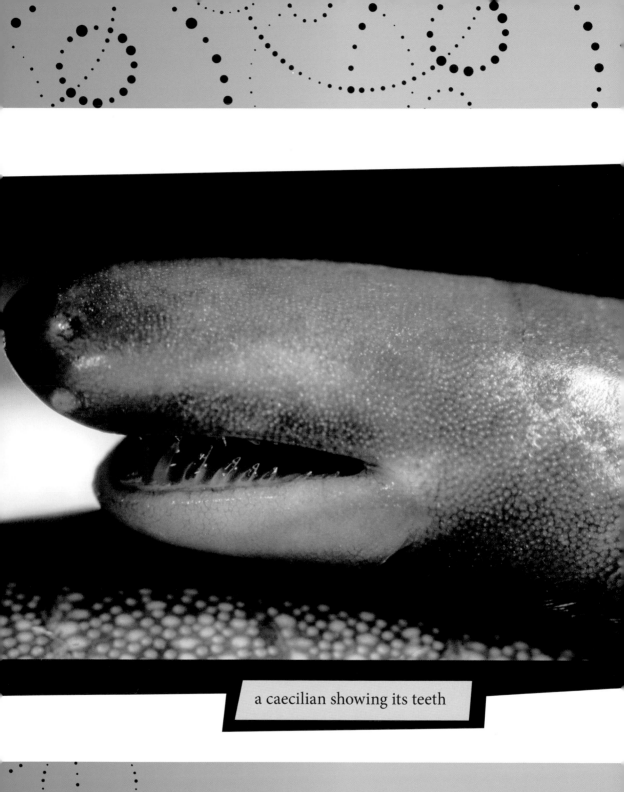

a caecilian showing its teeth

CHAPTER 4

Unusual Behavioral Features

Wood Frogs

Wood frogs start out life much like other frogs. Tadpoles hatch from eggs in the water. They go through metamorphosis after about two months. They turn into adult frogs and move to land.

Wood frogs are found in the northern United States, Alaska, and Canada. Winters can be very cold. These frogs have a special way of surviving the icy temperatures. They find logs or leaves to hide under. They **hibernate** there through the winter. They stop breathing. Their hearts stop beating. More than half of the water in their bodies turns to ice. When spring comes, the wood frogs start breathing again. Their hearts start to pump. Their bodies thaw and they hop away.

HUGGING HOPPERS

Many animals can tell males and females apart by sight or smell. But not wood frogs! Male wood frogs don't know which ones are females. During **mating** season, they have to hug other wood frogs to see if they are fat. Females carrying eggs are fatter.

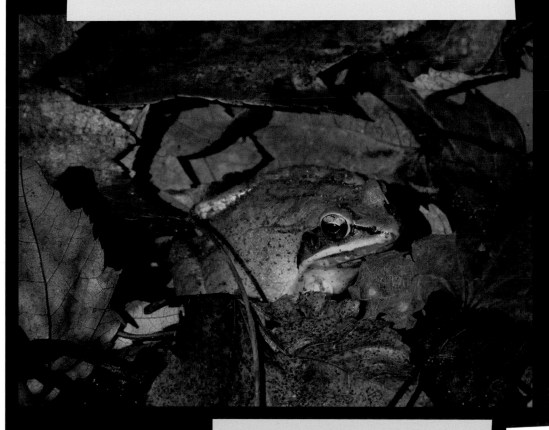

Wood frogs hide from predators such as snakes, foxes, and raccoons.

Glossary

algae (AL-jee)—small plants without roots or stems that grow in water or on damp surfaces

amphibian (am-FI-bee-uhn)—a cold-blooded animal with a backbone; amphibians live in water when young and can live on land as adults

clone (CLOHN)—to make an exact copy of something

digestive system (dye-JESS-tiv SISS-tuhm)—the group of organs responsible for breaking down food into energy for the body and for getting rid of waste

gill (GIL)—a body part on the side of fish and some insects that allows them to breathe underwater

hibernate (hi-bur-NAYT)—to spend winter in a deep sleep

larva (LAR-vuh)—an animal at the stage of development between an egg and an adult; larvae is plural for larva

mate (MAYT)—to join with another to produce young

metamorphosis (met-uh-MOR-fih-sis)—the series of changes some animals go through as they develop from eggs to adults

predator (PRED-uh-tur)—an animal that hunts other animals for food

prey (PRAY)—an animal hunted by another animal for food

tentacle (TEN-tuh-kuhl)—a long, flexible limb (like a leg or an arm) used for moving, feeling, and grabbing

Read More

Amstutz, Lisa J. *Amazing Amphibians: 30 Activities and Observations for Exploring Frogs, Toads, Salamanders, and More.* Chicago: Chicago Review Press, 2020.

Jacobson, Bray. *Amphibian Life Cycles.* New York: Gareth Stevens Publishing, 2018.

Klepeis, Alicia Z. *Nature's Undead: Snapping Rattlesnakes, Frozen Frogs, and Other Animals That Seem to Rise from the Grave.* North Mankato, MN: Capstone Press, 2017.

Internet Sites

Ducksters: Amphibians
ducksters.com/animals/amphibians.php

Home Science Tools: Life Cycle of a Frog
learning-center.homesciencetools.com/article/life-cycle-frog/

SeaWorld Parks & Entertainment: Axolotl
seaworld.org/animals/facts/amphibians/axolotl/

Index